4|10|12

All About America

THE INDUSTRIAL REVOLUTION

Hilarie N. Staton

KINGFISHER
NEW YORK

All About America: THE INDUSTRIAL REVOLUTION
All rights reserved. No part of this book may be reproduced or utilized in any form or by any means, electronic or mechanical, including photocopying, recording, or by any information storage or retrieval systems, without permission in writing from the publisher.

LONDON & NEW YORK

Copyright © Bender Richardson White 2012

Published in the United States by Kingfisher,
175 Fifth Ave., New York, NY 10010
Kingfisher is an imprint of Macmillan Children's Books, London.
All rights reserved.

Distributed in the U.S. and Canada by Macmillan, 175 Fifth Ave.,
New York, NY 10010

Library of Congress Cataloging-in-Publication data has been applied for.

ISBN paperback 978-0-7534-6670-4
ISBN reinforced library binding 978-0-7534-6712-1

Kingfisher books are available for special promotions and premiums. For details contact: Special Markets Department, Macmillan, 175 Fifth Ave., New York, NY 10010.

For more information, please visit www.kingfisherbooks.com

Printed in China
10 9 8 7 6 5 4 3 2 1
1TR/0911/WKT/UNTD/140MA

The All About America series was produced for Kingfisher by Bender Richardson White, Uxbridge, U.K.
Editor: Lionel Bender
Designer: Ben White
DTP: Neil Sutton
Production: Kim Richardson
Consultant: Richard Jensen, Research Professor of History, Culver Stockton College, Missouri

Sources of quotations and excerpts
Page 6, reporter's quote: Hindle, Brooke, and Steven Lubar. *Engines of Change: The American Industrial Revolution, 1790–1860*, page 49. Washington, DC: Smithsonian Institution Press, 1986. Citation is Schöpf, Johann David. *Travels in the Confederation, 1783–1784*, volume 1, page 30. Translated by Alfred J. Morrison. Philadelphia: W.J. Campbell, 1911.
Page 6, Thomas Jefferson quote: http://etext.virginia.edu/jefferson/quotations/jeff1320.htm
Page 17, advert source: www.maine.gov/sos/arc/sesquicent/transcpt/batesmill.html
Page 23, Ford quote: Ford, Henry. *My Life and Work: An Autobiography of Henry Ford*. [S.l.]: BN Publishing, 2008.
Page 27, Roosevelt announcement: http://docs.fdrlibrary.marist.edu/od2ndst.html
Page 29, Roosevelt letter: www.loc.gov/teachers/classroommaterials/presentationsandactivities/presentations/timeline/depwwii/wwarii/fdr.html

Acknowledgments

The publishers would like to thank the following illustrators for their contribution to this book: Mark Bergin, James Field, Nick Hewetson, John James, and Gerald Wood. Map: Neil Sutton. Book cover design: Neal Cobourne.
Cover artwork: John James.
The publishers thank the following for supplying photos for this book: b = bottom, c = center, l = left, t = top, m = middle
© The Bridgeman Art Library: Collection of the New-York Historical Society p13br, 16cl, 18br; Peter Newark Pictures p19br • © Getty Images: p14tl, 14bl, 16b • © Library of Congress: pages 1, 2–3, 30–31, 32 (LC-DIG-pnp/pan.6a04417), 20tl (pnp-cph.3b03834/LC-USZ62-55956), 20–21 (LC-DIG-nclc-04457) • © TopFoto.co.uk: The Granger Collection, New York City/TopFoto pages 4tl, 4bl, 5br, 7tr, 7br, 8tr, 8bl, 8br, 10tr, 11tl, 11cr, 11bl, 13tl, 13bl, 13br, 14br, 15tl, 16–17, 18bl, 20bl, 20br, 21cr, 22c, 22br, 24tl, 25cl, 26–27, 27tr, 28tl, 29t, 29c.
Every effort has been made to trace the copyright holders of the images. The publishers apologize for any omissions.

Note to readers: The website addresses listed in this book are correct at the time of publishing. However, due to the ever-changing nature of the Internet, website addresses and content can change. Websites can contain links that are unsuitable for children. The publisher cannot be held responsible for changes in website addresses or content or for information obtained through third-party websites. We strongly advise that Internet searches should be supervised by an adult.

CONTENTS

Introduction

The Industrial Revolution looks at how new ideas, inventions, and improvements in technology changed everyday life in the United States from around 1750 to 1950. It shows how almost everything once made slowly, by hand and often at home, became mass-produced quickly by machines in factories and mills. The machines were powered first by people or horses, then by running water, steam, electricity, and oil. As industries grew, so did trade, business, towns, and cities. The story is presented as a series of double-page articles, each one looking at a particular topic. It is illustrated with paintings, engravings, and photographs from the time, mixed with artists' impressions of everyday scenes and situations.

In Colonial Times

Made in their homes or imported

During the Industrial Revolution, people developed new machines and products. They switched from working at home to working in factories and stores and on canals and railroads.

When Europeans came to North America, starting in the 1500s, they found rich soil, forests, animals, and the American Indians. They cleared the trees off the land and planted crops. They had to make their own tools, as well as anything else they needed, or they had to have it brought by ship from Europe.

Britain set up 13 colonies on the eastern coast of North America. Because the people living in the colonies were British subjects, they had to follow Britain's rules. The British government told its American colonies that they could trade only with Britain. They were also told that they could not make certain goods in the colonies but instead had to buy them from Britain, making that country wealthy.

▲ Colonists used simple tools to do complex tasks such as building and repairing ships.

▲ Colonial shoemakers often made their own leather for their shoes.

▼ Colonial metalworkers had to pound their material by hand to make dishes and tools.

▲ A colonial American blacksmith forges weapons at the outbreak of the American Revolution.

◀ Tailors

▶ Furniture maker

Made by Hand

Colonists made goods by hand. They made everyday items such as candles, clothes, and furniture. A few people, called craftspeople, made things that needed special skills. Some made shoes, others guns, and a few made cloth. Their workshops were parts of their houses. Whatever the colonists did not need for their own use, they sold to other colonists or traded for goods from other people. They might have traded or exchanged candles for cloth, or meat for a chair.

U.S. industry around 1850

Cotton
Corn and wheat
Sugar
Rice
Tobacco
Textiles
Factories and mills

N

▲ The Industrial Revolution was centered on towns and cities in the eastern and northeastern United States. This revolution saw major changes to the production of food, clothes, and machinery.

The American Revolution

Beginning in 1763, the British government placed new taxes and trade controls on the 13 American colonies. The colonists objected to this because they wanted to run the colonies themselves and make their own decisions. As taxes increased, the colonists grew angrier. Battles broke out in 1775. In 1776, colonial representatives wrote the Declaration of Independence. This document said that the 13 colonies were now a free country. Britain and the colonists fought many battles until 1781. Finally, in 1783, Britain recognized the United States as an independent country.

New manufacturing methods

Technology had helped Americans win the Revolutionary War. During the war, an American company used new metalworking skills to make a huge iron chain to stop the British navy from sailing up the Hudson River. A factory in Pennsylvania made rifles that fired more accurately than British rifles.

Making Cloth

Colonists used wool from sheep and fibers from the flax plant to make cloth. Women often cleaned the fibers and used a spinning wheel to spin them into thread. A machine called a loom wove the threads together to make cloth.

A Trading Nation

American trade unleashed after independence

The United States could now make, buy, and sell whatever it wanted or needed. With a new type of machine and more slaves, more cotton was grown and sold. Ships took American cotton and other goods all over the world and returned with manufactured items.

After the war, many aspects of life changed greatly, but others stayed the same. In 1784, a farmer–tavern keeper told a recorder, "I am a mover, a shoemaker, furrier, gardener, wheelwright, farmer, and when it can't be helped, a soldier. I make my bread, brew my beer, kill my pigs; I grind my axes and knives. I built those stalls . . ."

The greatest change was in the farming industry, which was boosted by slavery—when one person owns another as if they were property. Large farms in the South, called plantations, had many slaves. Plantations usually grew tobacco or cotton to be sold. These crops took a lot of work to grow. Slaves were expensive to buy, but they worked for no pay and had no freedom. Because slaves did not cost much to keep, many plantation owners became rich by selling their crops.

Government and Trade

The new government encouraged U.S. citizens to start industries and to trade with other countries. Thomas Jefferson, the third U.S. president, wanted Americans to grow crops instead. But by 1809, he had changed his mind and wrote, "The spirit of manufacture has taken deep root among us, and . . . [is] too great . . . to be abandoned."

▼ **After the war with Britain, ships from many countries arrived with manufactured goods.**

America's Shipping

Sailing ships imported, or brought in from other countries, goods such as manufactured glass, iron tools, and cloth. They also imported slaves from Africa. They exported, or shipped overseas, lumber, tobacco, and other natural goods. Rum was the only manufactured export.

◀ The homemade barrels used to ship tobacco weighed about 500 pounds (225 kg).

Crops, Farmers, Slaves, and Cotton

Starting between the late 1600s and early 1700s, indigo (a blue dye), rice, and tobacco were grown as major crops in the southern United States. They were sold throughout the colonies and to many overseas countries. Farmers spent many hours planting, weeding, picking, and getting these crops ready for market. After the invention of the cotton gin, many southern farmers switched to growing cotton. Plantation owners bought more slaves so they could plant more cotton to sell. By the 1830s, cotton was the United States' biggest export.

The Industrial Revolution arrives

The first major technological change of the Industrial Revolution happened in the South. Eli Whitney built a machine called the cotton gin in 1793. It helped farmers remove the seeds from the white, fluffy cotton bolls much quicker than could ever be done by hand. A man could clean only one pound (0.45 kg) of cotton a day by hand, but with a cotton gin, he could clean 50 pounds (23 kg) a day. Cotton production soared, with most of the work done by slaves. Wealthy southern farmers sold the cotton in New England and in Britain, where it was manufactured into cloth.

▲ Eli Whitney's cotton gin used a metallic brush to pull out the sticky seeds from the cotton fibers.

7

Powered by Nature
Industry expands and speeds up

As technology changed, wood and flowing water were used as fuel to power developing industries. Wood and water were also necessary for a new power source—steam. Steamboats moved people and goods faster.

▲ U.S. cargo ships took goods all over the world. They were built from lumber and powered by wind blowing their sails.

American farmers grew a lot of wheat. At first, each farmer used a horse to turn a big, flat stone to grind wheat into flour. Then gristmills—places that ground wheat into flour—were built on rivers with fast-moving water. The water turned a wheel that rotated the mill's grinding machine and ground the wheat much faster. Huge mills shipped flour to American and European cities. Sawmills used water power to run the large saws that cut trees into lumber. People used lumber to build homes and ships, and some of the lumber was exported, making sawmill owners rich.

Using several different inventions, Oliver Evans developed a new type of flour mill that made producing large amounts of flour even easier. In his automated mill, machines did all the work, overseen by one person.

War of 1812

In 1812, another war broke out in North America between the United States and Britain. It was over land in Canada and the fact that Britain was forcing U.S. sailors to serve in its navy. The war lasted almost three years. During this period, people in the United States had to live off whatever they could make for themselves. The war hurt U.S. trade but strengthened its textile industry because there was no imported British cloth.

▼ In 1785, Oliver Evans's automatic flour mill took wheat, ground it into flour, and then put it into barrels.

Shipbuilding

Shipbuilding was an important industry in New England. This part of the country had thick forests with plenty of wood, but its shipyards had to import metal tools, equipment, and manufactured sailcloth. Each ship took a long time to build because the work was done by hand.

▶ Flour mills that were
wind-powered worked
only in a steady wind.

New power arrives

In England, by 1780, a new type of moving force—steam
power—was being used on a grand scale. In 1807, American
Robert Fulton powered a boat with an English steam engine.
Early steam engines burned wood that heated water to make
steam. More and more steam created a pressure that made the
engine turn. Soon steamboats were taking goods and people
up and down rivers all over the United States. In time, steam
engines burning coal would be used to drive railroads, farm
machinery, and factory pumps.

Machines Do Their Share

The Industrial Revolution in the
United States was centered in the
East because that is where most
people lived. But there were not
enough people to do all the work,
so Americans invented machines to
help them work faster. The cotton
gin and Oliver Evans's automated
flour mill needed fewer workers but
did more work. Steamboats traveled
faster and carried more goods than
smaller sailboats.

▲ Water power was used
to run flour mills (main
image), machine shops
(above), and sawmills
(right). Building mills
and workshops near
water allowed finished
goods to be carried
away easily by boat.

The First Mills

Factories are set up for mass production

The textile industry was the first to be transformed by the Industrial Revolution. It used new technology to make large quantities of cloth faster than people could make it by hand. Factories were set up alongside rivers and canals in New England.

The American colonists grew cotton, but they did not have the technology to turn it into textiles, or woven cloth. Instead, they sent their cotton to British textile factories, or textile mills. The British kept their textile technology secret, but in 1789, English-born Samuel Slater brought it to the United States.

▼ Workers left their farms to live in houses near the textile mills where they worked.

Weaving

George Washington proudly wore a suit of "homespun" cloth when he became the first president of the United States. The cotton fibers were raised in the southern states, spun into thread, and put onto a loom, maybe like the one above. They were woven into cloth, and the cloth was sewn into a suit.

▶ Textile mills had a wheel outside that was turned by water currents. Using gear wheels and drive belts, power from this wheel was used to turn machines inside the mill. On the first and second floors, machines prepared the cotton or wool, spun it into yarn, and then wove the yarn on looms. On the top floor, the finished cloth was bundled for shipping.

▼ The first American textile mill was built by Samuel Slater in Pawtucket, Rhode Island, in 1793.

New England's textile factories

In Massachusetts, Slater improved on the British spinning machines. He built textile mills near Boston that used water power to run the spinning machines that made yarn. The yarn was then sent to local families, who used their own looms to weave it into cloth.

New England's textile industry grew quickly. By 1814, Francis Cabot Lowell had built a factory in which the cotton was spun into yarn and then put on power looms, which wove it into cloth. Cotton was brought into the factory, and the finished cloth was shipped out. Machines did almost all the work.

▼ Adult workers ran many power looms at the same time. Children fixed the thread when it snapped.

The Mill Day

Most textile mill workers were young women and children. They arrived at the mill before the sun was up and did not leave until after dark. They worked six days a week, often 12 hours a day. Inside the factory it was cold and drafty or hot and humid. The air was filled with dust and lint. Sometimes workers were hurt by the machines. Mill workers worked hard for little money.

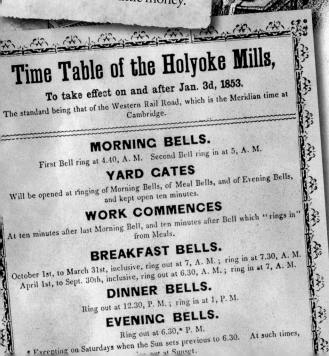

Time Table of the Holyoke Mills,

To take effect on and after Jan. 3d, 1853.

The standard being that of the Western Rail Road, which is the Meridian time at Cambridge.

MORNING BELLS.
First Bell ring at 4.40, A. M. Second Bell ring in at 5, A. M.

YARD GATES
Will be opened at ringing of Morning Bells, of Meal Bells, and of Evening Bells, and kept open ten minutes.

WORK COMMENCES
At ten minutes after last Morning Bell, and ten minutes after Bell which "rings in" from Meals.

BREAKFAST BELLS.
October 1st, to March 31st, inclusive, ring out at 7, A. M.; ring in at 7.30, A. M.
April 1st, to Sept. 30th, inclusive, ring out at 6.30, A. M.; ring in at 7, A. M.

DINNER BELLS.
Ring out at 12.30, P. M.; ring in at 1, P. M.

EVENING BELLS.
Ring out at 6.30,* P. M.
* Excepting on Saturdays when the Sun sets previous to 6.30. At such times, . . . at Sunset.

Mill-working life

Most textile workers came from New England farms. Many were young women who lived in a boarding house while they worked in a mill. They were not used to being paid or having someone watching everything they did. They had to follow company rules even when they were not at work. After a few years, most returned to the family farm. Eventually, the mills hired immigrants who had newly moved to the United States. Many immigrants wanted to build better lives for themselves and were prepared to do hard work for little pay.

◀ Many New England textile mills had a rigid schedule that the workers had to follow.

11

Canals and Factories

Moving materials and products

The United States was so big and the land so unsettled that moving goods was an expensive problem. Better roads, new water routes, and railroads were built to move goods to and from factories. As transportation improved, cities and industrial centers developed.

◄ **In 1829, the Stourbridge Lion was the first engine in the United States to pull cars, but it only ran one time because the tracks could not support the train.**

▼ **The Erie Canal had 83 locks to raise and lower the water and canal boats.**

Factories needed good transportation so that materials could reach them and so that their finished goods could reach buyers. There were some good local roads but only one good major road west—the National Road. There was no easy way to get people or manufactured goods from northeastern factories to midwestern cities. As a solution, private companies built man-made waterways, called canals, to move goods. At first, short canals helped only local businesses. Then, in 1825, the 363-mile (584-km)-long Erie Canal was opened. People and goods could now be moved easily and cheaply from the Northeast to the Great Lakes.

▼ **Canal boats were pulled along slowly by horses or mules that walked alongside on towpaths or slopes.**

Erie Canal Opens New Markets
Settlers and goods were taken by steamboat up the Hudson River to Albany, New York, and on to Buffalo along the Erie Canal. From Buffalo, they traveled across the Great Lakes to Detroit, Michigan. Grain from the Midwest arrived in Buffalo, traveled the Erie Canal, and was then shipped down to New York City. There, it was used, shipped to other cities, or exported.

Railroads transport goods

Starting in the 1830s, the United States imported British steam-powered railroad engines and laid tracks throughout the Northeast. Soon, railroads were carrying goods to and from lakes, canals, and factories. By 1860, trains ran from the East to Missouri. With better transportation, the Industrial Revolution spread to cities farther west.

Manufacturing the American way

In 1798, Eli Whitney developed another breakthrough technology: a new way of manufacturing guns. Skilled workers made interchangeable parts that almost anyone could fit together to build or repair the guns. This type of manufacturing became known as the American system of production.

Clocks were mass-produced in this way, too. A traditional clockmaker might build three or four clocks a year, but a factory worker using the new system could make hundreds of clocks in the same period. Factory owners made so many clocks that they sent peddlers to farms and villages to sell them.

◀ Women operated power looms that sent shuttles like these back and forth 100 times a minute.

▲ Side view of William Horrocks's Power Loom, used in the factories of Lowell, Massachusetts

LOWELL OFFERING

December, 1845.

A REPOSITORY OF ORIGINAL ARTICLES, WRITTEN BY "FACTORY GIRLS."

LOWELL: MISSES CURTIS & FARLEY. Boston: Jordan & Wiley, 121 Washington street. 1845.

◀ Women working at the Lowell textile mills wrote poems and articles for magazines such as the *Lowell Offering*.

▲ Factories such as the Stillman & Allen Novelty Iron Works were built along waterways because heavy goods had to be shipped by water.

13

Natural Resources

Making the most of its raw materials

The speed and power of the Industrial Revolution in the United States was a result of the country's wealth of fertile land, huge forests, and vast deposits of minerals such as coal, iron ore, gold, silver, and petroleum.

Natural resources are the trees, lands, water, and minerals that people use to make and do things. In 1805, President Thomas Jefferson sent Meriwether Lewis and William Clark on an expedition to see what natural resources were in the West. They found many forests and rich farmland, as well as a route to the Pacific coast. Later, pioneers discovered valuable minerals in the ground and major waterways in the West.

In the late 1700s, large deposits of the mineral coal had been discovered in Pennsylvania and Virginia. Coal is important because it can be burned to create heat and steam power. Factories and railroads were built near the coal mines, and new cities grew around them. The Industrial Revolution continued to spread across the country.

▲ The first miners used basic technology, like a pickax and shovel, to find silver and gold.

Precious Metals

In 1849, gold was discovered in California, and more than 100,000 men joined in the rush to mine it. The Colorado silver rush followed soon after. Most miners used hand-powered tools to collect loose gold and silver. Soon, large mining companies took over and used more advanced technologies to find the buried metals.

◄ Large mining companies bought out small miners.

▼ Coal miners worked deep underground in dangerous and unhealthy conditions.

Coal, the Fuel of Industry

During the Industrial Revolution, coal was burned to create steam to power machines and fuel railroad engines. Coal was also burned to heat iron so that it could be made into machines, railroad tracks, and tools. Factories no longer needed to be built near fast-flowing water for power and transportation, and many canals became disused.

Iron and petroleum

The metal iron is obtained by heating iron ore. In the 1840s, huge iron ore deposits were found in Michigan and Minnesota, but it was hard to get the ore to iron mills in Pennsylvania and Ohio. Finally, railroads from the mines and steamships on the Great Lakes made it easier. The iron was made into machines and machine parts. Soon, new technology was invented to make the iron into steel, which is an even stronger metal.

Another major natural resource, crude oil, or petroleum, was discovered in Pennsylvania in 1859. This black liquid was pumped out of the ground by oil wells. Factories called refineries made the oil into kerosene, which was burned in lamps. By the 1890s, gasoline, which is made from refined petroleum, was being used to fuel the newly perfected internal combustion engine.

Whale Oil

Whaling ships traveled from New England to hunt whales in the dangerous northern Pacific and Arctic oceans. Sailors in small whaleboats shot the whales with harpoons. Once a whale died, they took the whale oil from the whale's blubber (its fat). This oil was used in lamps, candles, and soaps and put onto machine parts to make them run more smoothly.

◄▲ Whale oil was used in lamps because it burned brightly and did not smell.

◄▲ During the 1850s, gold miners developed several new ways of mining.

Industrial Strength

War leads to a growth of industry

Problems between the industrial North and cotton-growing South caused Americans to fight one another. The Civil War and the rebuilding afterward boosted industry so fast that this period of U.S. history has been called the Second Industrial Revolution.

◀ Women went to work in factories to replace the men who joined the military.

▼ In 1862, the USS *Monitor* was the first ship covered with iron to join the U.S. Navy.

In 1860, the North said that free men, not slaves, should do the work. The South insisted on using slaves and tried to break away from the United States. It formed a separate country, called the Confederate States of America, and went to war with the North. It lost a bloody civil war, which lasted from 1861 to 1865.

The North had many factories, railroads, canals, and farms. It had coal and iron, too. It was able to supply everything its military needed. The South did not have enough natural resources or factories to provide what its military needed. This was a deciding factor in the war.

Industry at War

In the North, government and industries worked together. Textile factories made cloth for uniforms. They ran out of cotton and switched to wool. Shoe factories made only boots for soldiers. The South did not have these industries, and many things had to be made by hand. Southern soldiers had to provide their own uniforms and shoes.

▶ Railroads carried messages, supplies, and soldiers during the war.

▼ Samuel Colt's factory made revolvers for the northern army.

▲ During the Civil War, iron mills introduced new technologies. After the war, additional technologies created a huge steel industry. Steel mills were built near Pittsburgh, Pennsylvania.

More workers needed

Because so many men went into the army, there were not enough people to do all the necessary work. Factories hired women, children, and new immigrants. During the war, the Bates Mill in Maine advertised for children as workers because of " . . . the inability of the Mills, to supply the Government with Tent Cloth. (So much needed by our Soldiers now in the field) . . . work 9 hours per day."

Peace brings industrial growth

After the Civil War, northern industries kept growing. New inventions and technologies created change in all parts of people's lives. Big industries and companies were founded, such as Andrew Carnegie's steel company and John D. Rockefeller's Standard Oil.

In the South, most people returned to cotton farming, but without slaves. They built railroad tracks and some factories. For a while, the Industrial Revolution raged in northern states but not in southern states.

Railroads—West Meets East

Americans wanted a transcontinental railroad—a railroad across the country. During the Civil War, a route was chosen. Northern factories made the iron railroad tracks, and immigrants laid them across mountains, through tunnels, and over bridges. When the railroad was finished, in 1869, trains brought the manufactured goods of the eastern factories to the western cities. They brought cattle from Texas and silver from Colorado to the Midwest and the East.

▶ On May 10, 1869, the transcontinental railroad was completed. The Union Pacific Railroad and the Central Pacific Railroad met at Promontory Summit, Utah, and the final spike was driven into the ground.

Phonograph

An Inventive Age

U.S. industry competes in the world

Starting around 1860, new inventions, increased scientific knowledge, and big businesses led to changes in energy production, transportation, and manufacturing. American companies began advertising and displayed their goods at world trade fairs.

Inventors tried to find ways to improve people's lives and tested many ideas before creating something new. Thomas Edison ran many experiments to create the best light bulb. Some inventions caught on more quickly than others: everybody wanted to ride the first Ferris wheel, but many people were afraid to have electricity in their homes.

Thomas Edison

Thomas Alva Edison worked on hundreds of ideas and inventions. He invented the phonograph—a type of disk player—and improved the movie camera and telephone, which other people had invented. He built laboratories where scientists experimented and formed companies to manufacture his products.

▶ In 1876, this Corliss Steam Engine was the world's largest steam engine and powered all the machines at Philadelphia's Centennial Exhibition.

Changing technology

New machines did jobs workers had once done or helped them do their jobs faster. Office and store workers became more efficient after the invention of the typewriter, telephone, and cash register.

Railroads became the most important way to move goods and people to and from cities, farms, factories, and mines. Trains speeded up delivery and lowered the cost of shipping. They allowed increasing numbers of settlers to move west.

Advertising

As factories made more of a product, they wanted to sell more of it. Companies—like the salt manufacturer below—began advertising so that people would choose their product over others. Ads helped introduce Kellogg's Corn Flakes cereal and Coca-Cola.

Early telephone exchange

▼ Iron and steel mills were built close to coal mines, railroad tracks, and rivers for ease of transportation.

▶ Worcester Salt advertising poster

WORCESTER SALT SPECIAL.
162 Cars started by President-Elect. William McKinley.

Agricultural Advances

New machines made farm work easier. Cyrus McCormick's reaper allowed a man to cut 12 acres (4.9 hectares) of wheat in a day instead of just one acre (0.4 hectare). John Deere's self-polishing steel plow did not get stuck in the mud. Barbed wire kept cattle out of fields, and steam tractors powered a range of farm machinery.

New industrial cities

Factories were built in Chicago, Illinois, because railroads met there on their way to midwestern farms and eastern cities. Trains brought cattle from Texas to Chicago and carried away canned meat. Minnesota's iron and Pennsylvania's coal were taken to steel mills in Cleveland, Ohio. Houston, Texas, became a railroad center, and cotton was shipped from there to textile mills in the Northeast.

In the 1880s, U.S. inventors Nikola Tesla, Thomas Edison, and George Westinghouse made electricity available to everyone. Soon, electricity was powering street lights and machines, creating a new world.

▼ Poster for the 1893 world fair in Chicago

ALL NATIONS ARE WELCOME TO THE WORLD'S COLUMBIAN EXPOSITION CHICAGO 1893.

Expositions

New inventions were displayed at world fairs or expositions. At London's 1851 Great Exhibition, Europeans were surprised at new U.S. farm machines. In 1876, at the Centennial Exhibition in Philadelphia, Americans displayed Alexander Graham Bell's telephone. Chicago's 1893 exposition gave a glimpse into how electricity could change life.

Industrial Giants

Unions, sweatshops, and the very rich

Business people started to use new inventions and technologies to run workshops and factories in cities. But they cared little about working conditions, so workers formed unions to try to improve their lives. Unions often clashed with the bosses.

▲ Wealthy businessmen lived in huge houses on New York City's Fifth Avenue.

In the early 1900s, technology changed cities in many ways. Electric lights lit the streets, offices, and homes. People traveled in electric streetcars, steam trains, and underground trains called subways. Steel girders supported tall buildings with elevators.

Both U.S. citizens and immigrants arrived in the cities looking for work. Unless they had skills, most began by doing the lowest-paying jobs. Some worked in factories, others at home. They were mostly paid not by the hours they worked but at piece rate—a few cents for each piece of an item they produced. Some sewed sleeves for coats. Others rolled cigars. Many workers found jobs in factories making steel or machines.

A Land of Extremes

By 1900, big businesses had grown into companies and were making their owners rich. Some paid their workers well. Many businesses relied on immigrant workers, whom they paid very poorly. These workers lived together in crowded apartments called tenements.

▼ In a food factory, children prepare vegetables to be canned.

► A 1911 cartoon of the Triangle shirtwaist factory fire disaster

Triangle Shirtwaist Factory Fire

A fire in New York City at the Triangle Waist Company on March 25, 1911, led to the deaths of 146 workers. Most were young immigrant women who sewed clothes for long hours in dangerous conditions. Locked exit doors and the absence of a fire alarm were responsible for the deaths. After the fire, many workers joined unions. New York State also passed laws to protect women and child workers.

▼ Groups of workers labored in small, cramped, dark rooms with no fresh air. Workshops and factories with unhealthy conditions were known as sweatshops.

Big businesses

As businesses used the latest inventions and technology, they became more successful. Big companies started to buy out smaller ones or force them out of business. Andrew Carnegie's steel company soon owned everything it needed to produce its steel: iron and coal mines, railroads, ships, and steel mills.

Many businesses got loans from banks. If a business could not repay its loan, the bank took control of the company. Bankers thus became industrialists, tying companies closer to those that financed them.

◀ Big houses on Nob Hill owned by men who built and ran California's railroads

▲ A cartoon showing two rich businessmen trying to save money by hiring workers for the lowest pay possible. The workers were being treated like slaves.

Immigrants, unions, and strikes

Millions of immigrants poured into the United States to take up work in its growing companies. Some of them formed unions— groups of workers who get together, or unite, to meet with their bosses to discuss changes for everyone. Since they were more powerful as a group, they asked for better pay, shorter working hours, and safer working conditions. Sometimes when company owners would not agree, workers went on strike, or refused to work. Sometimes the government brought in the police to end a serious strike.

The Nobs of Nob Hill

Nobs were the richest of the rich. They got that name because in San Francisco, California, they build their mansion houses on Nob Hill. These men built and ran railroads or struck it rich in Nevada's Comstock silver rush. Many of their huge houses were destroyed in the 1906 San Francisco earthquake and fire.

Mass Production

U.S. industrial strength grows

By 1905, factories across the United States were turning out huge quantities of a large range of products. Soon new types of engines, fuels, and production methods would further change industry in dramatic ways.

In a factory, most workers made just one part of a product many times a day. Other workers put the parts together to complete the product. This system, called mass production, allowed factories to produce large amounts of goods more quickly and cheaply than the old method, in which one worker made a whole product on their own. Mass production was used for canning food, manufacturing trains, and making interchangeable parts to go into bigger products. Because factories could produce so many identical items efficiently, each one could be sold at a low price.

◀▼ **Workers used new technology to make iron and steel into huge machines.**

Steel Production

Steel is made from iron but is harder and more flexible. It is also more complicated to make. In the mid-1800s, two new ways of making steel were invented. Because the United States had large amounts of coal and iron, steelmaking was a major industry. As more was made, the price of steel dropped from $160 ($3,300 today) per ton to $17 ($460) per ton from 1875 to 1898. Steel was used to build railroads, machine parts, and tall city buildings.

▲ **Steel from Homestead Steel Works was used to make the rails for railroads and to build skyscrapers.**

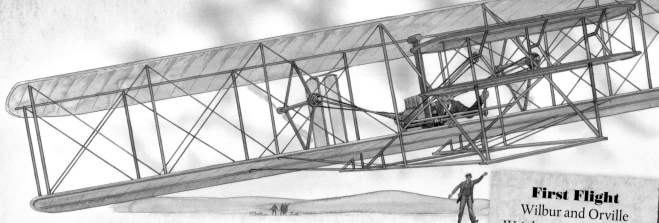

A new engine, a new way of working

In the 1890s, inventors built an engine that used gasoline to produce power. It was called the internal combustion engine. Then, in 1901, an oil boom started at Spindletop, Texas. New oil refineries were built near Houston to make cheap gasoline to power the new engines. Since the city was close to the Gulf of Mexico, the gasoline was sent by tanker ships to other parts of the country.

Industrialist Henry Ford improved mass production by creating an assembly line. Each worker in his automobile factory did something different to the car as it was moved along, such as adding a tire or fitting a seat. In his autobiography, Ford said, "The first step forward in assembly came when we began taking the work to the men instead of the men to the work."

▲ In 1903, the Wright Brothers from Dayton, Ohio, become the first to fly a plane that the pilot controlled.

▼ Every car that came off Henry Ford's assembly line was exactly the same. Other companies copied his production methods.

First Flight
Wilbur and Orville Wright studied flight and also knew how bicycles and engines worked. They analyzed problems and figured out how to solve them. They went to Kitty Hawk, North Carolina, to test their plane designs. Their first controlled flight lasted less than a minute, but it began the aircraft industry.

Ford's Car Production Line
Henry Ford developed a way to move cars along an assembly line. Unskilled workers stood on either side of the line to assemble, or put together, the cars from interchangeable parts made in factories. In 1909, the Model T car cost $850 ($21,000 today), but in the 1920s only $260 ($2,800).

Progress and War
Technological changes speed up

In April 1917, the United States was drawn into a world war. This boosted industry and opportunities for work and allowed women to push for the right to vote.

Before the war, huge construction projects were already using many new technologies. In New York City, Chicago, and St. Louis, skyscrapers, bridges, and tunnels were built using steel skeletons. New York City built a huge earth dam to hold back water, flooded a valley, and laid pipes to bring the water more than 100 miles (160 km) to the city. Skilled architects, engineers, and craftsmen were paid to work with and supervise unskilled workers.

At the same time, the oil industry developed around Cleveland, Ohio, and spread to Texas, Oklahoma, and California. The automobile industry grew rapidly in Detroit, Michigan. Seattle, Washington, became a major seaport and center for making aircraft. Industry had now reached all parts of the United States.

◄ A 1909 painting of building Manhattan Bridge in New York City

Riding into Modern Times

After Henry Ford introduced his Model T car in 1908, millions of people could afford a rugged, reliable, and simple automobile. They soon demanded better roads and highways and used service stations for gas and repairs. Car owners started touring and taking longer vacations, which led to the growth of resorts and the motel industry. Then General Motors expanded the market with an installment plan, allowing people to buy a car by paying a little of the cost each month.

THE STANDARD OIL CO. AUTO FILLING STATION

DRIVE IN SLOW

DRIVE IN SLOW

▲ Standard Oil service stations providing gas and repairs were set up across the country.

▼ New technology was developed during World War I (1914–1918) so that airplanes could use guns to fight one another. Planes were also used to find out what was happening on the ground and sometimes to drop bombs.

Inventions and advances in communication

Scottish-born U.S. scientist and engineer Alexander Graham Bell invented the telephone in 1876. It was developed from the telegraph. Whereas the telegraph sent electrical coded messages along wires, the telephone sent voice messages over the wires. By 1900, many businesses and homes had a telephone, and long-distance communication across the United States expanded rapidly.

Scientists knew about radio waves, but it took many inventions and improvements before this "wireless" communication was practical. The first radio station began broadcasting in 1920. Radios received news and music nationally and from other countries. The telephone and the radio changed the way people exchanged information.

ON THE JOB FOR VICTORY
·UNITED STATES SHIPPING BOARD·
EMERGENCY FLEET CORPORATION

Helping Its Allies

World War I was fought in Europe. At first, the United States only sold war goods to help its allies (friendly nations), Britain and France. Then, in 1917, the United States joined the war. It provided ships, soldiers, money, food, and raw materials such as chemicals and steel. Partly as a result of its war effort, U.S. industry soon became one of the most successful in the world.

Women's Rights

U.S. women had been asking for the right to vote, called suffrage, for many years. Then, during World War I, women successfully did many jobs that only men had done before. Because of this, President Wilson supported their plea for the right to vote. Finally, in 1920, the Nineteenth Amendment to the U.S. Constitution was approved, giving women the right to vote.

VOTE
WOMEN'S VOTE NOW

▲ At suffrage marches, thousands of women and men marched in support of giving women the right to vote.

◀ During World War I, women were the drivers for officials, a job that had never been open to them before.

25

From Boom to Bust

Financial crisis leads to the Depression

In the early 1920s, industry was booming and cities were exciting places to live. But within a few years, everything came crashing down. In the 1930s, government programs helped restore industry and jobs.

In the 1920s, new technology was widely used in factories, on farms, in offices, and at home. Almost everyone who wanted a job was able to find one, and workers were better paid than ever before. Most people were getting richer, and even poor people managed to survive. Then, in 1929, an economic depression began. A depression is when business activity drops. Many people could no longer afford to buy goods, so factories stopped making them and workers lost their jobs. By 1932, more than 23 percent of workers were out of work. Farmers also had problems, including bad dust storms.

▼ During the Depression, many people were said to "have to make do and mend."

Roaring Twenties

In 1920, for the first time, more U.S. citizens lived in towns and cities than in the countryside. In cities, they enjoyed music, dancing, movies, and shopping. Department stores and mail order catalogs sold mass-produced refrigerators, clothes, and furniture.

Banks Crash

Many Americans had saved their money in banks. The banks loaned the money to farmers and businesses. With the Depression, the loans went unpaid. As savers tried to get their money out, the banks shut down. Many people lost their savings. Others had to wait months to get their money back.

▲ Many Oklahoma farmers left their farms and traveled to California in hopes of finding work and a new life.

The government steps in

Soon after Franklin D. Roosevelt was elected president in 1932, he began to help ordinary people, farmers, and businesses. He set up a series of programs called the New Deal. Some programs set rules for banks and other businesses, while others created jobs and hired many workers. One project oversaw the building of huge dams. These made electricity, protected land from flooding, and provided water for farmers and cities.

In 1936, President Roosevelt again promised to help workers and businesses: "The government . . . will continue . . . to improve working conditions . . . reduce hours . . . increase wages . . . end the labor of children . . . wipe out sweatshops . . . support collective bargaining . . . [and] stop unfair competition." Within a year, U.S. industry had started to recover.

▲ During the Depression, people who were out of work kept going to factories and stores looking for a job. Many who had a job had their pay cut.

▶ Many New Deal programs put people to work.

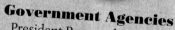
A WPA PROJ

Government Agencies

President Roosevelt created several government agencies to carry out his New Deal programs. The Public Works Administration created jobs to build roads, airports, and bridges. The Social Security Administration started a program that would give people a pension when they retired from work at age 65. The Federal Deposit Insurance Corporation protected money in banks. The Tennessee Valley Authority built dams that made electricity.

▲ The Works Progress Administration hired photographers to take pictures of the harsh living conditions during the Depression.

New Industrial Age
From the Depression to modern times

World War II ended the Depression as factories began hiring workers again. New discoveries and technology helped increase output from industry and save lives, but it also created the power to destroy people and places.

▲ During World War II, government posters praised women workers.

In 1939, Germany sought to take control of Europe and went to war with Great Britain and France. The United States tried to help its allies but did not want to fight. Then, on December 7, 1941, Japan made a surprise attack on the U.S. fleet at Pearl Harbor. Angry Americans went to war against Japan and Germany and worked hard to produce planes, ships, and tanks for 12 million U.S. soldiers. Many men left their jobs and joined the military. Millions of new workers found jobs in factories and even moved to a new city to work. They included many women and African Americans who had never before worked in a factory.

Industry Steps Up

After joining the war, the U.S. government required that industries stop making goods to sell to people and that they make only war goods. Instead of cars, automobile factories made trucks, jeeps, and even guns and airplanes. Farms and the food industry had to sell much of what they produced to the military. Shipbuilding grew quickly and mass-produced many ships for the U.S. Navy.

Science to Bomb

In 1942, in Chicago, scientific discoveries l[...] to a secret governmen[...] project, the Manhatta[...] Project. Scientists work[...] on a bomb that was so terrible the governmen[...] hoped it would end the war. Once it was tested, two atomic bombs were dropped on Japan. These caused massive destruction but ended the war in Asia.

▼ The aircraft industry soon became the biggest industry in the United States.

▲ Many women built airplanes and ships during World War II.

New technology

Science and new technology helped win the war. In 1943, President Roosevelt wrote to a scientist working on the atomic bomb: "Whatever the enemy may be planning, American science will be equal to the challenge." New U.S. planes were larger, faster, and more powerful than ever before. Radar used radio waves to locate enemy craft that previously could not be seen. A new medicine, penicillin, stopped infection of war wounds.

After World War II, U.S. industries produced more than any other country in the world. They supplied other countries with steel, jet planes, food, and clothes. They used new technology to improve cars and to build a television industry. They went up into space and deep into the ocean. Although the Industrial Revolution is long over, U.S. citizens continue to use technology in new ways.

The secret Manhattan Project developed and tested the atomic bomb during World War II.

▲ After the war, most U.S. families owned at least one car and used it as their main means of transportation.

▲ Real-estate developer Bill Levitt used mass production to build well-made houses.

Postwar Technology

New technology changed life following the war. Nuclear power plants started producing electricity using the same technology that led to the atomic bomb. The first modern computers, each the size of a room, were used to handle large amounts of data. Rockets were built that took satellites into space and, eventually, people to the Moon and back. Medical advances helped millions live longer and happier lives.

Glossary

assembly line a factory line where something is moved along while workers add interchangeable parts to it until the product is complete

canal an artificial waterway on which boats move, carrying people and goods

coal a black rock that is burned to create heat

colony a place under the control of another country

experiment to try out ideas many times with small changes to see what will work best

export to send goods out of a country to be sold

factory a building where workers use machines to make products for sale

immigrant a person who has come from another country to live and work

import to bring goods into a country to be sold

Industrial Revolution a time during which there were many major improvements and advances in how and what type of goods were made

industry a group of businesses that make, sell, or provide one type of good or service

interchangeable parts parts that are exactly the same so they can be switched out easily in a finished product

invention something new that is created by doing repeated experiments

inventor a person who studies, experiments, and creates something new or improves on another's ideas

iron ore a mineral that, when heated, makes the hard metal iron

kerosene a product of petroleum that is burned for heat and light

loom a machine used to weave threads together to make cloth

machine a device that helps a person do a specific job better, faster, or easier

manufacture to use tools and machines to make quantities of a product to sell

mass production making large amounts of the same product

military the fighting forces of a country—the army, navy, and, in modern times, the air force

mill a place that produces a product, often flour or cloth; an early factory

mineral a natural solid substance

natural resources the things in nature, such as minerals and water, that people use to make products or create power

petroleum a black liquid that is pumped out of the ground and is used to make kerosene, gasoline, and other products

revolution a time of great change

steamboat a boat with an engine powered by steam

steam engine an engine that uses wood or coal to heat water to create steam that powers its moving parts

steel a metal that is made when iron is treated as it is heated. It is stronger and more flexible than iron.

technology the way people make tools and how they use them to make other things they want and need

textile cloth made from cotton or wool

union a group of workers who join together to improve their working conditions and pay

Timeline

1712 First steam engine invented in England

1721 First factory set up in England

1763 Efficient steam engines developed in England

1775–1783 The American Revolutionary War

1779 A steam-powered textile mill is built in England

1793 Eli Whitney develops the cotton gin

1793 Samuel Slater builds the first successful water-powered textile mill in Pawtucket, Rhode Island

1801 Eli Whitney delivers muskets made with interchangeable parts to the U.S. military

1807 Robert Fulton runs the first steamboat

1809 The United States stops trade with Britain, so U.S. textile mills produce more cloth

1812 War of 1812 stops European imports, so U.S. factories produce more goods

1817–1825 The Erie Canal is built in New York State

1831 The first railroad in the United States to use a steam engine pulls freight and passengers cars

1835 Samuel Colt invents the revolver

1837 John Deere develops the steel plow

1844 Samuel Morse invents the telegraph

1847 Cyrus McCormick begins mass-producing his reaper

1852 and 1855 William Kelly and Henry Bessemer invent processes for mass-producing steel

1861–1865 The Civil War halts cotton exports and encourages northern industrial development

1869 The transcontinental railroad is completed

1876 Alexander Graham Bell invents the telephone

1879 Thomas Alva Edison invents a light bulb

1884 The first skyscraper is built in Chicago, Illinois

1892 Andrew Carnegie founds Carnegie Steel Company

1903 Wilbur and Orville Wright make their first successful powered flight

1908 Henry Ford introduces the Model T car

1914–1918 World War I; United States joins in 1917

1929 The Depression begins

1933 President Roosevelt's New Deal programs start

1941 The United States enters World War II; U.S. industry and farming focuses on the war effort

1945 The United States drops atomic bombs on Japan, ending the war in Asia

Information

WEBSITES

Energy Kids, U.S. Energy Information Administration, History of Energy
www.eia.doe.gov/kids/energy.cfm?page=4

The Henry Ford museum: Model T Road Trip
www.thehenryford.org/exhibits/smartfun/welcome.html

History of modern communications technology
www.fcc.gov/cgb/kidszone/history.html

National Child Labor Committee's collection of photographs
www.loc.gov/pictures/collection/nclc/

Railroad Museum of Pennsylvania
www.rrmuseumpa.org/index.shtml

Samuel Slater's Pawtucket, Rhode Island, textile mill
www.woonsocket.org/slater.htm

BOOKS TO READ

Bartoletti, Susan Campbell. *Kids on Strike!* Boston: Houghton Mifflin, 1999.

Bender, Lionel. *Invention*. New York: DK Children, 2005.

Brezina, Corona. *The Industrial Revolution in America: A Primary Source History of America's Transformation into an Industrial Society.* New York: Rosen Publishing Group, 2005.

Hillstrom, Kevin. *The Industrial Revolution*. Detroit, MI: Lucent Books, 2009.

Krull, Kathleen. *The Boy Who Invented TV: The Story of Philo Farnsworth.* New York: Knopf Books for Young Readers, 2009.

Mitchell, Don. *Driven: A Photobiography of Henry Ford.* Washington, DC: National Geographic, 2010.

Index